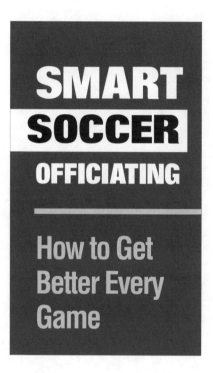

SMART SOCCER OFFICIATING

How to Get Better Every Game

by Carl P. Schwartz,
Referee Contributing Author

Cover design by Lisa Martin
Graphics by Carrie Kwasniewski
Edited by Julie Dus

Referee Enterprises, Inc.,
Franksville, Wis.

SMART SOCCER OFFICIATING:
HOW TO GET BETTER EVERY GAME
by Carl P. Schwartz

Copyright © 2001 by Referee Enterprises, Inc,
P.O. Box 161, Franksville, Wis. 53126.

Printed in the United States of America

ISBN 1-58208-022-4

Kevin Stott,
California

Table of Contents

Introduction

This book is slightly different than those I've written in the past. The goal is to discuss some techniques that might be useful to you as you progress in your referee career. The goal is to expand the vision with which you look at the game.

How is that possible? Managing the game's restarts is the fundamental element you need for game control. Without mastering that vital component, players and spectators will not accord you the respect needed to become an accepted referee. Start with the basics, and get them right.

There are other aspects of the game you need to get right. The professional-division referees heard about four critical calls to get right in their contests. Just four calls? Yes, pretty much. If you get those four calls right, the rest follows.

The next two chapters tease your imagination. With the intriguing title of "Are You a Cheat?" we wanted to pose some questions for you to ask yourself. While you think you're doing the game a greater justice by slipping in your own interpretation here and ignoring a Law there, you are not. You may be a cheat — a cheat with all the right intentions, of course. Sometimes those personal interpretations or those overlooked Laws take on a life of their own. Some grow to mythical proportions. Louisiana's Bob Wertz, a master at thinking about the game, implodes a few of those myths. He gives you the myth, the background and a plausible explanation to help you train others about the correct interpretation.

The first two chapters talk about making the right calls. But perhaps more important is making the right no-call. (Dan Heldman hates it when I say that because there are several categories of no-call. More properly called call-sorting, no-calls range from contact that is not a foul, through contact that is a trifling or doubtful foul [and thus not whistled], to fouls that are observed but go unwhistled due to an advantage to one player or team. I'll use the common term "no-calls" to include all three.) Top referee administrators scour the country for great referee candidates. Know what they're looking for? Beyond someone who has the basics down (dress, timely arrival, concentration, fitness, hustle), they are looking for someone who knows when not to blow the whistle. While you can't master that technique by reading a single chapter, M.C. O'Bryant's "No Harm, No Foul" would be that chapter if it were possible.

If you are not already near the top of your avocation as a referee, you probably vary your age groups from weekend to weekend. Maybe even within the same weekend, you'll do a mix of U-10, U-14 and U-18. Those are very different contests. If you are not making the needed adjustments, or don't know what adjustments need to be made, David Keller's chapter is key to your continuing education.

There are many people to thank in the writing of this book. Celebrating the birth of his first granddaughter while proofreading this text, Dan Heldman continues to contribute to *Referee* and NASO in an unmeasurable way. Authors Jonathan Meersman, Bob Wertz and David Keller are friends, advisors and great people to have on your side. Although I do not know Mr. O'Bryant personally, I admire his writing. There is much to learn from his work.

Herb Silva is a great personality within the game. Much of his wisdom is reflected in these pages.

And although their words are not directly reflected in these pages, the education I gained over the years from Stanley Lover and Pat Smith are the guiding lights I've used to both write and edit the material. Thank you both.

Good luck in your games ahead.
Carl P. Schwartz

1

Mastering Restarts

By Jonathan Meersman

Roger Sill,
Florida

Mastering restarts is a key to improved refereeing. The efficient use of your whistle, signals, body language and a few key words can do much to improve game control and player management. Watch professional-level referees work matches on television. Watch top collegiate referees in your area. Make arrangements to speak with them after the game and ask them about certain aspects of their restart management that you witnessed.

Many goals occur as a result of dead-ball restarts. Some cite statistics as high as 40 percent of all goals come from the first touch or two after restarts. Therefore it is crucial that you correctly administer restarts — throw-ins, goalkicks, corner kicks and free kicks. A great deal of dissent and ill feelings toward you can be prevented by being close enough to sell the call, and by reacting quickly and confidently.

> **Some cite statistics as high as 40 percent of all goals come from the first touch or two after restarts. Therefore it is crucial that you correctly administer restarts.**

Out of bounds

When the ball travels completely over the boundary lines of the field (other than under the crossbar and between the goalposts), a goalkick, corner kick or throw-in restarts play.

For you to award one of those restarts, you must determine that the ball is indeed out of play, you must know which team last touched the ball before going out of play, and you must know which line the ball went over. That information determines the manner by which you restart the game quickly and correctly. For valid goals, a kickoff restarts play, regardless of which team touched the ball last.

Unlike most sports, in soccer the ball is out of bounds regardless if it left the field on the ground or in the air. Even if the ball curves back into the field of play before hitting the ground, it is out of play. Award one of the three restarts.

Dealing with restarts after the ball goes out of play should be very simple. When the ball goes out of play, react quickly and decisively. Assistant referees in the diagonal system of control (DSC) need to give crisp and confident signals according to the rules or Laws and specific to your pregame instructions.

Assistant referees usually make recommendations for calls in their own quadrants of the field. You generally make the call in your quadrants, but should look to your assistant referees for help in case of uncertainty.

Although NFHS rules allow you to administer a dropped ball if you are unsure of which team caused the ball to go out of bounds, that method should be used sparingly. Reliance on dropped balls gives players, coaches and spectators the impression that you weren't paying attention. Make decisions and live by them. Young referees sometimes drop balls to hide behind a lack of courage to make a firm decision. Even first-year officials should simply make a ruling and continue with the game. Don't invite criticism. In a USSF match, *do not* restart with a dropped ball due to your indecision.

If you are unsure, read the players' body language. In many cases, they tell you in their own way what the correct decision should be. Is one team running to pick up the ball while the other team is retreating? Which way did the ball deflect? Use your listening skills. Did you hear the ball strike a player? Did you hear a second touch? Is one player saying to a teammate, "You'll get it next time, Mike." That's a clue to give it to the other team. Although knowing which team caused the ball to go out of bounds is the best option, you can sometimes read the players and avoid dissent.

If you are working with assistant referees, look to them for assistance. Even if you are closer to a play, use your assistant referees when unsure. When all else fails (your decision, help from the assistant, players' body language), the current attacking philosophy of the game suggests that you give the ball to the offense.

The field must be equipped with corner flags. Those are in place to assist you in some close situations. If the ball strikes a corner flag and stays on the field, the ball is considered inbounds.

Throw-ins

When the ball goes out of play over either touchline, a throw-in is awarded to the team that did not touch the ball last. The throw-in must be taken from near the spot where the ball passed over the touchline (one yard in all directions).

If the players are unsure of the throw-in location, point it out. Use a short chirp on your whistle if they don't see your signal. If the throw-in is taken from an improper spot, award a throw-in to the opponent at the spot where the ball initially went out of play. Give the players the benefit of the doubt.

When officiating younger players, it is especially important for you to make sure throw-ins are executed properly. As players become older and develop their skills, throw-ins become routine, with a few exceptions.

Sometimes, the ball hits the line or breaks the plane of the line in the air, then immediately goes back out of play and the assistant referee points the flag for a throw-in for the same team. That is wrong. If the ball goes inbounds then out, the throw-in goes to the other team. Under NFHS rules, even if the ball does not enter into play directly from a throw-in, award a throw-in to the opponents.

Players cannot be declared offside if they receive the ball directly from a throw-in. The throw-in ends at the instant the ball breaks the plane of the touchline (and leaves the player's hands, if appropriate).

Opponents have no distance requirement to obey during a throw-in. Opponents must not jump up and down or wave their arms to impede a throw or distract the thrower. In that instance, the offender must be cautioned for unsporting behavior. If the referee's decision to caution precedes the throw-in, the restart is the throw-in. If the ball breaks the plane of the touchline before the referee makes the decision that a caution is warranted, technically, an indirect free kick restarts play. You have some flexibility based on when you make your decision, as opposed to when you whistled.

Divide throw-in responsibilities between yourself and the assistant referees during the pregame discussion. For instance, some referees watch the ball and the release and instruct the assistant to watch for foot violations. Some referees prefer to watch the entire throw-in and ask the assistant to watch where the ball is expected to land — looking for holding, pushing, flying elbows, etc.

Goalkicks

When the ball travels entirely over the goalline, having last been touched or played by the attacking team, award the defending team a goalkick. Any player on the defensive team may take the goalkick, which may be taken from anywhere within the goal area. That removes one possible source of time wasting.

During a goalkick, the ball must completely leave the penalty area and enter the field before it is in play. If the ball touches any player or leaves the field before leaving the penalty area, the goalkick must be retaken. Older players generally have no trouble putting the ball into play. In games involving younger players, you should be in position to make sure the ball clears the penalty area. Attackers must remain outside the penalty area until the ball is in play.

In the DSC, use your assistant referees; they might have a better view of the ball. They should signal the ball out of play according to the rules or Laws and your pregame instructions. During the pregame conference, confer with your assistant referees to watch for proper ball placement. Then they should move to a position even with the second-to-last defender to judge offside on a counterattack. Also ask them to make sure the ball comes into play properly when you are not near the penalty area.

With older players, position yourself close to the ball's anticipated landing area, or "dropping zone." You need to read each game, and each kick, to know what your best position will be. Don't watch the ball; watch the players. Their eyes and bodies tell you where the ball will land or if you are in the way of the play. Be close enough to convincingly call pushing, holding and other fouls, but not so close as to interfere with play.

Corner kicks

When the ball travels entirely over the goalline and the defensive team played it last, award a corner kick to the attacking team. Any player from the attacking team may take the corner kick. The place where the ball rests on the ground must be in the arc or on any of its boundary lines on the side that it went out of play.

Because corner kicks may result in a goal directly from the restart, your assistant referee must be in position even with the goalline to judge whether or not a goal is scored. If the ball crosses the goalline — in the air or on the ground — and travels back into play, it should be declared out of play and a goalkick (or goal) should be awarded.

Imagine instances in which the ball curves out of play and then back into play, then an attacker heads it into the back of the net. Thousands of fans are going crazy for the apparent beautiful goal. As an assistant referee, raise your flag to declare the ball out of play before the goal. The most important thing to remember if that situation happens to you — raise your flag or blow your whistle *immediately* when the ball curves out of bounds.

Defenders must remain at least 10 yards from the ball until it is in play. You, or your nearest assistant referee, should make sure that the defensive team allows the proper distance. Be firm, but polite to the players. Do not physically back them away from the ball. Point to a spot; use your voice or use your whistle to get the 10 yards for the offensive team.

> **The most important thing to remember if that situation happens to you — raise your flag or blow your whistle *immediately* when the ball curves out of bounds.**

Vary your position during corner kicks. Never be in the way of the players or the goal area, but be close enough to watch them. Moving to different positions on subsequent corner kicks is a good preventive-officiating technique. Players are less apt to foul if they know you are watching them. Keep the players wondering where you are at corner kicks. You can actually see them looking for you.

Keep a close watch on goalkeeper B1 and attackers who stand just in front of B1. The attacker, if standing still, is permitted to be in that position. A player may not move around and impede B1. B1 may try to take control of the situation by pushing or holding the attacker. Talk to the players in that situation — it prevents ill feelings or fouling. By simply being present and letting your presence be known, you can prevent fouls and misconduct. More experienced referees will tell you, "Presence lends conviction. That advice helps your game management dramatically.

Free kicks

Properly dealing with free kicks (direct or indirect) can be a challenging experience for even the most talented officials. There are many factors for you to consider when a foul or other infraction results in a free kick. There are also many game management strategies to remember to get the game restarted quickly and fairly for both teams.

When you award a free kick, the ball must be placed near where the infringement occurred. There are a few exceptions: a penalty kick; a kick for the defending team in the goal area, in which case the ball can be placed anywhere within the goal area; or an indirect free kick for the attacking team in the opponent's goal area, in which case the ball is placed on the goal area line, parallel to the goalline, at the point nearest to where the infringement was committed. Manage the distance between where the incident occurred and the restart location with a dose of common sense. Six inches outside the opponent's penalty area? The two locations ought to be pretty close. In the defensive half — 80 yards away from the goal being attacked? Several yards is a reasonable distance.

For any free kick to be taken correctly, the ball must be stationary and all opposing players must be at least 10 yards from the ball (in all directions).

The wall

If the attacking team wants to take a quick kick before the opposing players have time to retire to the proper distance, allow play to continue. If the defense decides to set up a wall, they must be at least 10 yards away from the ball. The exception: if an indirect free kick is awarded to the attacking team within 10 yards of the goal, defensive players may be closer than 10 yards only if they are standing on the goalline and between the goalposts.

When you assist in setting up the wall, keep one eye on the ball. The kicking team may try to advance the ball if you are not watching. It is a good idea to move laterally to watch both teams. You should be able to spot 10 yards immediately, without pacing it off. Use field markings. *Never turn your back on the ball.*

Be decisive and consistent when calling encroachment. In order to penalize players for encroachment, you need to understand common characteristics associated with the infringement. It involves restarts and it is done intentionally to delay the restart of the match or to change and restrict the angle of the ball's direction so as to provide greater protection for the defenders' goal. Failure to penalize encroachment demonstrates lack of game control. The resulting dissent leads to frustration for both you and the players.

Participants perceive encroachment as lack of your quickness and firmness. They direct their anger at your authority. Encroaching players may be cautioned according to the rules and Laws. Dealing with the first instance helps your game management greatly. Be firm. Be forceful. Get a minimum of 10 yards on your first wall and the rest get easier. If you find yourself still dealing with walls late in the second half of any contest, you need to improve that aspect of your game.

The free kick begins with a signal from you. The signal may be a blast of the whistle, a beckoning or similar motion of the hand or a verbal, "Play it." If a quick kick is taken, the signal to take the kick could be the same as the one you used to stop play for the infringement. If there are problems dealing with a wall and the attacking team has requested their 10 yards, instruct them to wait for your signal, usually a whistle. If they do not wait, bring the ball back and retake the kick.

Indirect free kicks

When an indirect free kick is awarded and the team takes a quick free kick, raise your arm straight above your head. The arm remains extended above your head until a second player plays or touches the ball or the ball goes out of play. That helps everyone recognize when a goal may legally be scored.

If the free kick is taken by the defense within their penalty area, the ball must also leave the area and travel onto the field before being played by another player. The penalty for violating that is a rekick, since the ball was not legally put into play. For the most part, coaches and players don't know that. So as they are shouting at you, simply direct a player to retake the kick and get the ball into play quickly and properly. The kicker cannot play the ball a second time until it touches or is played by another player of either team. If the kicker violates that rule or Law, an indirect free kick is awarded to the opposing team. The exception is if the ball has not been properly put into play. On a free kick within their own penalty area, players may not touch the ball a second time inside the penalty area. A rekick would result in that case.

With either type of free kick, it is possible for attacking players to be guilty of an offside infraction. You or the lead assistant referee must be in line with the second-to-last defender to judge potential offside infractions. Many defensive flat-back fours try to create an offside trap during free kicks. They move up just before the kick is taken to force the attackers into an offside position. Be alert for that tactic.

Dropped balls

Because dropped balls are rare, it is important to know which rules or Laws apply to the match you are working. A dropped ball occurs after a temporary suspension in the game and when any other type of restart would not apply (injury, weather, outside agent, etc.).

The spot for the dropped ball is where the ball was when play was suspended. If the ball was in the goal area, it is dropped on the goal-area line parallel to the goalline nearest to where the ball was when play was stopped. NFHS rules require two opponents to be present for the drop; FIFA Laws and NCAA rules have no requirement. *Advice to Referees* 8.5 offers additional guidance.

Make sure the players are far enough away from the drop site so you avoid being struck by the ball. If players are present, remind them the ball must touch the ground before it may be played. Drop the ball straight down from waist level.

Restart Fundamentals

• A team taking a free kick may not score directly on itself.

• The player taking the restart may not play the ball again until it has touched or been played by a player of either team. If the player does play the ball a second time successively, an indirect free kick is awarded to the opposing team at the site of the violation.

• Throw-ins and indirect free kicks must touch or be played by another player from either team before a goal can be scored. If the ball goes directly into the opponent's goal, award a goalkick to the defensive team. If a throw-in or indirect free kick taken from outside the penalty area goes directly into the team's own goal, award a corner kick to the attacking team.

• A player may not be declared offside directly from a throw-in, goalkick or corner kick. But, offside applies to any subsequent pass.

• During restarts, don't forget there are still 21 other players on the field. If the ball is played far off the field, use the time while the ball is being retrieved to scan the field. Make sure the players know that you are looking around. Watch players around the ball's anticipated landing area for pushing, holding or other fouls that can occur while players are jockeying for the best position to play the ball. Make eye contact with both assistants.

• On any kick, the ball must be kicked and move to be in play. The distance the ball must move has not been defined by a minimum distance. Use common sense and allow play to continue.

• A direct free kick is a restart after one of the major fouls. If the major foul is committed by the defense within their penalty area, award a penalty kick. An indirect free kick is the restart after a technical foul. That kick cannot lead directly to a goal; the ball must be touched or played by another player, besides the kicker, before a goal may legally be scored.

(Jonathan Meersman is a NISOA and USSF official, as well as an assessor and a high-level instructor. A native of Ohio, he and his soccer-referee wife now live in Milwaukee. Meersman serves as Referee's *"Doing It" columnist.)*

2

Four Critical Decisions

By Carl P. Schwartz

Zim Boulos, Florida

USSF PHOTO

There is a concept being widely discussed among former and current professional referees. Understanding it will help you become a better referee regardless of the game level you work. Get these four decisions right and your game will improve.

I first heard the concept mentioned at one of the eight Professional Division clinics offered by USSF manager of professional division assignment and assessment Herb Silva. Silva was a professional referee for many years in the Major Indoor Soccer League and a top collegiate referee. He now heads up the team of 130 National Assessors that view and report on the performances of 220-plus national referees at the professional division (MLS, WUSA and the United Soccer League's A-League, D-3 and W-League). No less an authority than Dr. Joe Machnik, former referee, formerly the U.S. Soccer men's national team goalkeeping coach and MLS vice president of operations, wrote about these four decisions in "The Right Call" in *USSF Fair Play*, Spring/Summer 2000.

What are the four critical decisions?

- Was the player offside or not?
- Was it a valid goal or not?
- Should the contact result in a penalty kick or not?
- Should the misconduct be penalized by a red card or not?

It seems self-evident that those are key decisions to your game management. At the professional level, as Machnik and Silva are concerned about, all the way down to U-10 recreational play, referees have to get those decisions right. Coaches, fans and players all ask for consistency — here is where the consistency comes in.

Level is significant

As you know from watching NBA, NHL and MLS contests, sometimes a certain level of contact is allowed at a professional-level match that might be whistled at a youth match. Given the player's skill, their temperament and ability to emotionally handle that contact and the skilled official's ability to read that the contact does not create a disadvantage, the contact goes unwhistled. So what you will read on these pages applies to upper levels of play. Those going from sub-varsity to varsity, those advancing into the collegiate ranks and those who are being prepared to work their first games in the professional division are the target audience.

Was the player offside or not?

Seems pretty simple. Heck, you learned all there is to know about offside in your entry-level clinic. Players who are in an offside position at the time of the pass from a teammate are liable to be whistled for an offside infraction. If they do not interfere, let play continue. If they gain an advantage, interfere with an opponent or interfere with play, the officiating team should penalize that infraction against the game. In concept, it is simple.

In practice, the dynamics of movement (see sidebar) play a large part in accurate decision-making. You need to be in position to make a believable decision. At upper levels, that position changes thousands of times during the game. Sometimes you might need to make an 18-inch adjustment to be perfectly positioned; sometimes you need to move 40 yards at top speed. But you need to make that position change. That involves fitness, attitude and concentration to the task at hand.

You've got to want to give the game 100 percent of your effort. You've got to want to give the players your best. If you're running the line and feel that you should be the referee, you will focus too much of your energy on watching play around the ball.

Your assignment for that game is to run the line. If you do your job well — get all your offside decisions correct and sell them via great positioning — the referee gets to focus on foul recognition and game management. If the referee is taking heat for your offside decisions, game management suffers.

You must adopt a standard philosophy toward penalizing offside. It must be the standard philosophy that the international community wants. It must be the philosophy that the International Football Association Board (IFAB) has decreed. It must be the standard philosophy that all three governing bodies in the U.S. have set forth. Dozens if not hundreds of times, the USSF has reemphasized that philosophy via its website to keep referees

---

An Assistant Referee's Dilemma

Suppose you're the assistant referee in a fast, competitive U-17 game. Because you anticipate some trouble, you're watching action around the ball when suddenly there's a long pass and you look to see an attacker chasing after the ball, about two yards beyond the defenders. The defenders are moving in the other direction in an apparent offside trap.

You wish you had been paying more attention to offside instead of to the action around the ball; however, a decision is still needed — offside or not?

Let's look at the physics of the situation. A fast U-17 player can run nearly 10 yards per second. A player starting from standing covers about half that in the first second, and a player running laterally can suddenly turn downfield and cover nearly 10 yards. Two players moving in opposite directions change their relative positions by the sum of their combined speeds, which means they can shift by 10 yards, even in the first second — as sometimes happens in an offside trap.

If you are watching play near the ball, it takes a fraction of a second to turn and then another fraction of a second to refocus and take in the play at the offside line. Even if the total time is only half a second, the players at the offside line may have changed their relative positions by five yards. Concentrating solely on the offside position and relying on hearing the pass can be better, but it still may take up to two-tenths of a second for the sound to reach you.

The moral of the story: Always know the relative locations of the players near the offside line. Then, even if you look away for a moment, when you return your attention to offside, you're updating a picture you already know rather than trying to build the scene from scratch. The difference is only a fraction of a second, but as we have seen, a lot can happen in that time. *(Jim Geissman is a soccer referee from Van Nuys, Calif. This article originally appeared in the 3/01 issue of* Referee Soccer Extra.*)*

informed. (All referees are invited to visit that site at
http://www.ussoccer-data.com/pubtopic.htm. Hit the "Get Topic
List" button and look for "Conference Call Notes" for what the
MLS and USSF leaders are telling MLS and WUSA referees.)

"When in doubt, leave the flag down." Professional-division
assistant referees who get their names in the paper do so because
they flagged an offside that wasn't. Their concentration wasn't
high enough. The intense focus needed to get the call right, at the
very high speeds of professional-division players, lapsed for a
split-second and they thought they would protect the defending
team. Video replays show their flags are improperly raised,
denying a legitimate offensive opportunity. At lower levels,
referees catch more abuse for not calling the offside than for calling
it. Thus assistant referees at youth contests tend to raise the flag
when in doubt. Once referees get in that habit, it is very hard to
reverse at higher levels. If your offside flag is often waved down
(average two or three times a game) because the ball goes to the
goalkeeper, your decision and flag are probably too quick. There
was no interference, there was no advantage gained. At the
professional level, two or three times a *season* would be too much.

There are cultures that still feel *any* player in an offside position
any time the ball is played forward *must* be flagged. Having been
trained via the USSF philosophy in the late 1970s, I took my
knowledge of the game to various parts of Europe in the '80s and
'90s. All was well until I started to officiate in top amateur and
semi-professional leagues in England. The English leagues had not
yet adopted that standard philosophy and there was a struggle, a
cultural clash. I survived that time, but the lesson is there for those
who still believe that any player in an offside position at the time
of a pass from a teammate is offside — you are in the wrong
culture to continue to hold that belief.

Believable and accurate offside calls come from focus and
concentration, holding a proper attitude toward the game, fitness,

positioning and having an accurate philosophy toward what the offside infraction really entails. Don't rush your decision. Don't rush your flag. "When in doubt, leave the flag down." If the Conference Call Notes can say it a hundred times, it bears repeating here.

Was it a valid goal or not?

Since the objective of the game is to score more goals than your opponent, that is a vital decision. Most of the goals you decide upon are very simple. As television announcer Tommy Smythe is fond of saying, the ball "winds up in the ol' onion bag." If the ball is delivered from a breakaway, a snap header or a half volley where there is no physical contact between opponents, you have a clear goal with no disputes.

Nearly every goalkeeper and defender who gets scored upon appeals for offside. It's becoming part of the game to make that appeal, however weak. So your first critical decision, offside, is a factor in your second critical decision.

Lots of Goals

The year 2000 saw the fullest schedule of internationals ever. While 48 percent of the 1043 matches were "friendlies," the competitive matches were up as well. Twenty-seven percent were World Cup preliminary matches, while 14 percent were continental qualifiers and 11 percent were continental finals (UEFA, COMOBOL, etc.).

Goals. Many non-soccer people complain about goalless matches. They say that indicates a lack of action. While it is true that 8.7 percent of the

Score	Percentage of Games with that Score
1-0	19.0
2-0	13.0
2-1	12.0
1-1	10.2
3-0	6.9
3-1	5.2

international matches had no goals scored, the following chart shows goals were scored — lots of them.
Source: 2/01 *FIFA Magazine*.

You can see from the sidebar that a single goal can be very important. Because of your association with the sport, you know that empirically. So you can imagine everyone's frustration when a goal is unfairly awarded or taken away because of an official's decision. Even if the decision in correct, it is going to be unpopular. If a coach or fan can show the mistake (over and over again) on videotape, not only is that individual referee going to face some criticism, but also referees in general will be lumped into that group. The fans will find some way to paint all officials with a broad brush.

Some decisions are correct, but the officiating crew doesn't sell them. Even if an assistant referee is perfectly correct in deciding that a ball was four inches more than 100 percent over the entire line before being bicycled out by a defender, the assistant can't sell that from 20 yards up the line. A different assistant, with the corner flagpost poking the right side of her ribs, is more likely to be believed — even if she is wrong. Location, position and the appearance of hustle are going to sell goals in controversial situations.

To this day, a 1966 World Cup goal awarded to England is disputed by all who don't inhabit the island-nation. A screaming shot hit the crossbar, drove quickly straight to the ground (no one denies at least part of the ball was over the line) and because of the spin on the shot, the ball rebounded out to the six-yard line. As the ball cleared to midfield, a raucous uproar forced the Swiss referee to consult his Russian linesman, who had been about five yards away from the corner flagpost. A couple of awkward moments, largely due to language differences, and a goal was awarded against the Germans.

Whether you choose to give the goal or not, you have to sell the goal. You may say that the goal doesn't have the importance of deciding a World Cup final. But if the goal you award causes team

A to go through to the U-14 semifinals, the crushing defeat to team B, it is their World Cup.

Referee columnist Jonathan Meersman was refereeing a contest where the assistant did not use the proscribed mechanics in *Guide to Procedures* 3I for a ball that was wholly over the goalline and returned immediately to play. Instead of coming to a stop, standing at attention with the flag straight up to request a stoppage and getting eye contact, the assistant simply made eye contact and began to sprint to midfield. Meersman, thinking the assistant was simply sprinting to stay with play, did not whistle immediately. After a few anxious seconds and a number of unpleasant (and unneeded) comments, Meersman stopped play, consulted with the assistant and awarded the goal. The assistant felt he had done the right thing by making "strong eye contact," in his words. Notice I said it was in the USSF's *Guide to Procedures* booklet. If you are working with a referee not trained by USSF (at a youth tournament, near a national border) that is probably the mechanic that referee will use. Make sure you are on the same page in your pregame discussion. Agree on a signal.

By not using the right mechanics, the assistant forced Meersman to sell the goal. Had the assistant followed the right mechanics, the assistant (who was perfectly positioned) could have easily and convincingly sold the goal. As it was, both Meersman and the assistant had to listen to comments from disgruntled fans and players for the remainder of the contest. That's why there is a standard mechanic — to quickly and unambiguously convey exactly what happened.

Sometimes you'll have to wipe out a goal. If you don't change anything about your normal mechanics, human nature is going to make it seem as if someone talked you out of the goal. Attacker A8 handles the ball off her upper arm into the goal, supposedly on the blind side of the referee. But the referee did see it. If the referee does nothing unusual — blows the whistle with the usual toot and points in the direction of the direct free kick restart — what's it going to look like? It's going to appear as if the referee missed the handling and is pointing to the center circle to award the goal. So team B is now unhappy. When the referee walks to the spot where the free kick should take place and tells B3 to take the free kick, suddenly team A realizes they are not going to get the goal — and they and their fans erupt, thinking team B talked the referee out of the goal. So the old adage, "You can only please half the people," is wrong. You've created a situation where *everybody* is mad at you and distrusting of your abilities.

As soon as you see the handling and realize it's headed for the onion bag, hit the heck out of the whistle. Do a Liberty Bell impression and try to crack your whistle with the blast. Although this is not an accepted signal under any code, extend, then cross your arms once or twice to show you are wiping it out immediately. Shout, "No, no goal" for those who aren't looking at you. Tap your upper arm once to show why you're denying the celebration and then show the direction of the restart. Any doubt as to what you're deciding? Any argument from anybody? Anybody think the other team talked you into something? Nope.

Just good clear communication regarding one of the four key decisions you have to make during the game. Hustle, be in position, use standard mechanics and use your tools (voice, whistle, hand and arm signals). That's selling your call. A valid goal is just one instance where you have to sell a decision. Another is …

Should the contact result in a penalty kick or not?

The world over, fans discuss the rightness (or the wrongness, if it's called against their team) of referees' decisions regarding penalty kicks. Whether you prefer the 82 percent scoring rate used in *Soccer Officials Guidebook* (based on research from *kicker* magazine in

Germany and the Portuguese and English soccer press) or the 94 percent that Bellion and Evans use in *For the Good of the Game*, a penalty kick affords a great opportunity to score.

There are many referees who choose not to award a penalty kick, stating that "I want the players to determine the outcome of the game, not one of my calls." That's a part of why the decision to award a penalty kick is so contentious. Too few referees award them. Particularly in the U.S., as young parents watch their children at youth games refereed by youth referees, they get used to some pretty horrendous contact in the penalty area with no resultant whistle. I say that not as a slam on U.S. fans or referees, but most Europeans and South and Central Americans grew up watching the game at the knee of their fathers and grandfathers and are slightly better able to differentiate contact that warrants a penalty kick. They have discussed it at length with someone who had intimate knowledge of the game. Perhaps colored by fanatic loyalty, at least the discussion helps those with long-standing affiliation with the game sort it out. At this stage in your life and your soccer officiating career, the only way you can make up for that lost time is to discuss foul recognition at your regular meetings, discuss it with mentors and assessors and watch games. Whether you are watching games with a whistle in your mouth or from your reclining chair amidst a group of other referees, discuss what you've just seen and hone your skills.

By Law (or rule in NFHS and NCAA), there is no differentiation in the amount of contact needed to call a foul at midfield versus what is needed within the penalty area. So, referees, if you call that shirt holding at midfield, and that same amount of shirt holding is going on in the penalty area, it should be a penalty kick. That's a pretty black and white view of the game. But it goes back to a paragraph at the opening of this chapter — level is significant. It is also why *Referee* sought reprint permission for Chapter 5 — "No Harm, No Foul." Chapter 5 very succinctly helps you appreciate the degree of contact that ranges from the trifling toward the foul.

But let's analyze the words of our ever-friendly referee who doesn't want to affect the outcome of the game via a penalty kick call. If the referee allows B4 to commit (substitute your favorite penal foul here, say tripping) against A9 just as A9 is about to shoot from a favorable angle and A9 does not get a shot, the referee *has* affected the outcome. If team A loses 2-1 because of that incident, the referee sends team A home just as if he had forfeited the match under NFHS or NCAA rules. That is not to say that every one of A9's shots is going to go in. Just as we say only 82 percent (or 94 percent) of all penalty kicks are successfully converted. But if A9 had a decent opportunity to play the ball and a team B player takes that opportunity away via a penal foul, the only way the referee can restore the balance is to award a penalty kick.

There is no need for the contact to be reckless for you to call a penalty kick. In fact, if the contact is reckless, it is both a penalty kick restart and a yellow card. If the contact uses excessive force, the restart is a penalty kick after you wait for the red-carded player to leave the field or surrounding area (based on player's age). It doesn't have to be "a good 'un" for you to call a penalty.

All referees have to do it; all referees have to become consistent. As a reader, you are probably a serious referee, dedicated to getting better. You might be a mentor, instructor, assessor or association leader. Here is where you have an opportunity to build consistency. At your meetings, talk about, "Should the contact result in a penalty kick or not?" Hash it out. Hear dissenting opinions. Bring film clips to discuss. Role-play actions in slow-motion so everyone can see it unfold piece-by-piece. Role-play actions three times — one definitely legal, one definitely foul and one where each referee has to be amidst the individual circumstances to make the decision.

Proper fitness, to be able to hustle to get close to the decision, is important. Moving to the proper angle to see the play is important. Sometimes you have to sacrifice closeness to the play to get the proper angle. Rather than running 10 yards right at the play, to put yourself 12 yards away, you might need to run at a 60-degree angle to the play, which will leave you 18 yards from play. But if you're 12 yards from play and looking at four players' backs and have to guess on what's going on, you can't sell your call. At top levels, if you are 18 yards away and the player who commits the foul blows off some verbal steam at you, simply ask, "Maybe, but did I get it right?" They'll usually nod and come over and pat your back. They know you need that angle.

Getting penalty kick decisions right is one of the four most critical calls you will make in your game. Be there. Decide on the elements of the contact. Decide whether the contact is trifling or puts the opponent at a disadvantage. Determine if you've been calling that level of contact in midfield — the penalty area is no place to tighten up from what you're allowing in midfield! Realize that your whistle doesn't affect the outcome of the game — you are simply restoring the balance created by a defender's penal action. One to go.

Should the misconduct be penalized by a red card or not?

That's a tough decision. Again, there are referees who will not issue a red card simply because it is a tough penalty — not only for the individual player, but for the team as well. As we discussed with penalty kicks, only discussions with senior referees and game experience will make your choices better. But let's look at some aspects.

If you keep your game data-wallet sheets, go back to past years. Analyze how often you send players off. One every 15 games, over the course of a couple of seasons? One every two games? Somewhere in there is an optimum number for you, given the tools you bring to the game and the level of competitive play you are working. If you are sending off a lot of U-12 players, you're probably in need of a mentor to help you better use the tools you have at your disposal. You probably need help in reading the game.

A NISOA National Referee may not have to send off a U-18 player all year long, but if you have five games of experience at that level, you may have four send offs in your first season. There are tools to use in lieu of a red card, in many instances. Pregame preparation, fitness, appearance, attitude, eye contact with assistants, voice, whistle, a quiet word, a public word, a stern look, hand gestures, a yellow card, a word with a third party such as a captain or coach and many others are at your disposal.

Don't misinterpret the paragraph above. You might very well be faced with a situation where you have to red card a player 12 seconds into the game. If you do it, (silently) thank the player for giving you a game-control gift, display the red card and send the amateur or professional player sight and sound from the field. (Youth players stay on the bench under the direct supervision of their coach. If the player still misbehaves, direct the coach to provide adult supervision for the player and record the name of that adult. Then send both sight and sound from the field.)

The Laws give referees great latitude in when to display misconduct cards. How you use that discretion speaks about game control. If you watch A4 spit on B7 and do not give the red card, you will have problems. Whether you give the red card or not remains your discretionary power, but you need to think about the consequences of not giving a red card that is needed, that is historically understood to be "an automatic." If you hear

A7 deliver a racial epithet toward the team B bench and do not hoist the right color plastic, the players will give you a much-needed lesson in game control. It may take them 10 minutes to do it. But if you let that epithet go with no punishment, expect that team A trainer to have to come tend to A7's injury within a short span.

The IFAB has set some red card offenses where you really have less latitude than others. Stopping an obvious goal-scoring opportunity by handling the ball is an offense against the game. In the '70s and '80s, that was a common offense. It has pretty much been stamped out via that IFAB edict. Players, coaches and fans have come to expect that red card, so referees don't take heat for it. The guilty player does, not the referee.

Stopping an obvious goal-scoring opportunity by an offense punishable by a free kick is another. There is a little wiggle room as to angles and exact location of secondary defenders, but if you've got a clear breakaway, you owe it to the game to play 10 versus 11. For some odd reason, many coaches think any penalty kick award has to involve a foul that denies an obvious goal-scoring opportunity, so every time you award a penalty kick, you must also show a red card. They usually think that when you call a penalty kick benefiting their team, not when their team committed the offense. That is one of the myths of the game!

We talked about spitting and how opponents will limit your options. Offensive language could be a topic for a whole chapter, if not a whole book. But there are some words or phrases, especially in some settings, that are deemed red cardable offenses. You lose all options on the second yellow card. Not sending the player off is a technical error on your part. Use your assistants and fourth official if there is any doubt or confusion. Even if it takes a minute or two of playing action for you to determine that A2 just got a second yellow, stop play when it doesn't put team B at a disadvantage and send off A2. Scotland's FIFA referee Hugh

Dallas had to do that during a game in Birmingham, Ala., during the 1996 Olympics.

But in reality, most red cards aren't given for those reasons. They are given for serious foul play or violent conduct. There you have much latitude. If the ball is in play, and the incident takes place on the field, committed by a player against an opponent while contesting for the ball, you have serious foul play. If any of those elements are missing, you have violent conduct. Be careful in reporting the facts, since some leagues penalize violent conduct more seriously that serious foul play — larger fines, longer suspensions.

Do you give a red card or not? There are dozens of factors to consider. Who committed the foul? Who was fouled? Was the fouled player a star? Was the fouled player the one who just scored the goal a minute beforehand? Where did the foul take place? What's the score? How far into the game is it? How many fouls has that player already committed? What is at stake — league title, local bragging rights? Are they graduating seniors who cannot be punished other than to have to leave this particular match (high school and NCAA, also U-19s who won't be playing amateur soccer)? Was excessive force used? (If it was only reckless, the players will feel cheated because the remedy for reckless play is a yellow card.) Perhaps more important than all those factors is the key question — Do I get something back in terms of game control by giving this red card? If the answer is yes, you have to give the card.

Four critical decisions. While you will make hundreds of decisions during the course of a game (Ball out? Throw to white or red? Is that enough contact to call a foul?), get these four right and your game control will improve. Players will respect your decisions more if you get these four right. You will hear less dissent if you get these four vital decisions right. You will feel comfortable at the competitive level you are working if you get those four critical decisions right. Administrators, assignors and assessors will recommend that you upgrade to a higher level of competition if you are getting these four key decisions right. It will take a short adjustment period at that higher level of competition — you may very well err on these four key points at that higher level, for a while. That's where a mentor and formal assessments come into play. Those tools speed the process by which you gain experience and assimilate the knowledge you gain at the new level.

3

Are You a Cheat?

By Carl P. Schwartz

Shannon Winston, Prince George, Va.

DALE GARVEY

A dmit it. When you saw the title, you were a bit offended, weren't you? Your reputation as a referee rests upon players, coaches and fans believing that you are fair and honest. They need to believe that you will give them a fair shake — make it a level playing field. Of course, they will voice an opinion when you don't call that contact against their star. Or when they feel that the yellow card you showed the defender was a bit harsh — the fans know that he would have settled down with a word from you. But as much as the game's participants and viewers complain to you, for the most part, they believe in your integrity.

So why the title of the chapter? An English publication, *The Football Referee* (similar to USSF's *Fair Play)*, asked a series of 22 questions of its readers on the topic. It's an interesting topic. Do we cheat as referees? Do we follow the letter of the *Laws of the Game* exactly? Where are your standards? What do you hold important? Something not addressed in England, because they don't have separate rules for high school and college competition, is adherence to the separate rules for each level of play.

It's an interesting topic. Do we cheat as referees? Do we follow the letter of the *Laws of the Game* exactly? Where are your standards? What do you hold important?

Use the following questions to explore your understanding of the game and your role in it. The original text is shown in italics. *Referee* guides some thoughts and reminds readers about national policy in standard text.

Do you turn a blind eye to contraventions of competition rules, such as late kickoffs, no corner flags, etc?
What time does the 8:00 a.m. game start? Because you are the opening game of an all-day tournament, you better get it started at 8:00. Not 8:04, not 8:10 because the star goalkeeper couldn't get out

of bed and get to the game site until 8:07. The tournament directors are counting on you to get the game going on time. The opposing team should not be penalized for being there on time.

Let's say it's the 2:30 p.m. contest on a blazing hot day. As you call for the teams at 2:29, team A comes right onto the field, standing around in the baking sun. The other team is standing there getting last minute instructions from the coach, each starter with an ice-water soaked towel over the head. Fair? When the tournament calls for a 10-minute halftime, do you wait until the full 10 minutes elapse before calling for the teams? Why not call them at eight minutes, allow them last-second instructions and a short team huddle and time to amble onto the field? Then you can blow for the start of the second half 10 minutes after you ended the first half.

As the referee, you do not have the authority to override competition rules. Follow them as written, much as if they were a part of the *Laws of the Game*. However, there are times you will want to act in concert with the tournament committee to set aside a rule. Let's suppose radar shows an approaching thunderstorm will be there in 70 minutes. You're supposed to play two 45-minutes halves. Meet with tournament staff and both coaches and for safety reasons, agree that the game will be two 30-minute halves with a four-minute halftime. That gives fans six minutes to get to safe cover.

Do you honestly think that players of offending sides at ceremonial free kicks are 10 yards away, or are you happy with eight yards?
If you only give the team eight yards, you are cheating. Law 13 clearly says, "all opponents are at least 9.15 m (10 yards) from the ball." You could ask them to step to 11 yards and that would not be against the Laws. There are two major reasons that you fail to get 10 yards.

The first is that you don't know how far 10 yards really is. From your playing days and early in your referee career, you felt you had a pretty good sense of what 10 yards looked like, so that's what you give. No referee instructor has ever tested your ability to judge 10 yards. Within Wisconsin, most referee instructors at entry-level and recertification clinics do a field exercise. Each participant is asked to bring something that is uniquely theirs (soda can, pen, eyeglass case or keys) to an open grass field. They are asked to stand in a very large semicircle around the instructor as the instructor places a ball in the center of the circle. Each participant is directed to move forward until they think they are 10 yards from the ball and place their unique object on the ground and then step away. One instructor holds the end of a 30-foot rope over the ball and the other instructor walks the semicircle showing exactly where 10 yards is. The exercise is repeated about 40 yards from the first site.

The first time, the average is about six yards. On the second exercise, the average is about eight and a half yards to 12 yards. A vast improvement for a 10-minute exercise, no?

The next reason is that you've tried to get full 10 yards and taken too much heat from the defenders. It just becomes easier to get eight and not have to listen to the complaints and comments. The attackers squabble a little when they only have eight, but nothing like the comments you have to hear to get those extra two yards. Is that cheating? Or taking the easy way out?

Are you allowing the attackers, who happen to be sitting on a one-goal lead, to request a ceremonial kick at every instance, even when the wall is set at 9.08 meters? Quickly judge that the wall is far enough and direct them to get on with play.

Have you ever failed to award a penalty because of the anticipated reaction it would cause from the defending team?
You would like to think not. But honestly, in your entire

officiating career you haven't overlooked a push when it was committed by one of Coach Jones' defenders? You all know Coach Jones. For 20 years, he's gained a (well-deserved) reputation for eating referees. So rather than listen to his long and loud tirade, you do not whistle the infraction. Is that fear? Is that cheating? Is that 20 years of the area's referees not taking care of business, allowing Coach Jones to grow into that formidable force?

Maybe you're being tested in a tough game. Game control is on the ragged edge, with team A leading, 2-1, and only 10 minutes left. You see significant contact by B4 in the area, but know that if you call the penalty kick, you are likely to lose all semblance of game control. You figure team A can hang on for 10 more minutes, so you no-call the contact (or worse yet, call for an indirect free kick or pull the restart out of the penalty area).

Have you ever knowingly allowed a saved penalty kick to stand, even if the goalkeeper moved forward, because it was a 'soft' penalty in the first place?

It wasn't a soft penalty because it was during kicks from the penalty mark, but the 1999 Women's World Cup final gives us an example of a referee not calling for a rekick. U.S. goalkeeper Brianna Scurry was well forward of the line before the kick. Did the Swiss referee cheat? More likely, she adhered to the standards she set for that level of competition. But do you have a tendency to give more latitude if you're uncertain of your most recent call?

Have you ever awarded a 'soft' penalty to cancel out a controversial award at the other end?

Referees all know there is no such thing as a makeup call, right? Try convincing television commentators and media that referees don't do it. But have you? Has there ever been a situation that, on its own merits, contact would have been considered trifling and would not have led to a whistle. But, taking into consideration that you gave a penalty kick at the other end 12 minutes ago, you decide to give the whistle a toot.

Equality is one of the three tenets of the game, along with safety and enjoyment. In Chapter 2, it was mentioned that some referees don't like to feel their calls affect the outcome of the game. That second penalty kick is a great balm for their feelings.

I won't say which culture the following story comes from, it's irrelevant. But the referees from that culture tend to meet separately with both coaches before the game — friendly tone-setting meetings. They find out who is near the top of the table, who is near the bottom of the standings. Inevitably, if the top-standing team is losing by a single goal with but a few minutes left to go — whistle, signal, penalty kick for the losing team giving them a chance to tie. Alternatively, should the teams be tied within the last five minutes, the defenders better stay well away because the slightest contact leads to a penalty kick to give the league-leaders their win. Cheating? As an assistant on those games, I sure thought so.

Have you ever cautioned a player for dissent, when he should have been dismissed for foul or abusive language?
Many, too many, players use "industrial language" as an adjective in describing what they think about your calls. For years, top referees were taught to distinguish between that sort of language talking about your calls (dissent and therefore a yellow card) and talking about you (offensive, insulting or abusive language and therefore a red card).

There is strong sentiment among referees to finish the game with 22 players. Sometimes, referees take that to an extreme. Sometimes, players are allowed to demean the referee's office with no action taken. Just like being too lenient with Coach Jones created a monster, many referees being lenient with foul language lends to a creeping problem. Rulemakers have to resort to zero-tolerance policies to fix a long-standing problem.

Top instructor Pat Smith, a member of several referee Halls of Fame, advocates taking care of vulgar dissenting comments in the manner they are made. If only you and the player speaking to you heard the words, you have hundreds of options. You can go straight to a red or yellow card, laugh, ignore the comments or any number of other things that fit the situation. If 10 players in the center of the field hear the comment, you better take care of business so at least those 10 players know you're taking action. It may be a card or it may be a comment, but you had better do something. If the player screams a vulgar remark in front of 2,000 fans from 70 yards, you had best deal with the comment openly and publicly. Anything less has two unwanted outcomes — you've given tacit permission for players to do it again and there will be erosion of match control.

Have you knowingly allowed a player to stay on by being lenient in dealing with a dismissible offense?

That goes back to referees being taught to finish a game with 22 players. That's a great goal! It truly is. But if A9 is hurting people by kicking them or striking them, A9 has to go. If A6 was cautioned for persistent infringement after holding opponent's jerseys six times, and still does it three more times, you have to get rid of A6. Anything less and the team B players will start to take justice into their own hands. That's not good for you. That's not game control. That's vigilantism. There is no safety, equality and enjoyment at that stage.

This is the one I will admit to. After 65 minutes, semi-pro team A was leading, 3-1. A4 began to dissent from every call. A4's behavior got progressively worse over the next 10 minutes. He wasn't hurting any team B players, but he was disrupting the game. He was disrupting his own team. So I calculated that if I left A4 in the game, he would be enough of an influence that team A would erupt. The final whistle found the score 4-3, to winners team B. Did I cheat? I didn't think so at the time. I thought I was taking a calculated risk. I was trusting that A4 would not take out his aggravation on a team B player's legs. But I was consciously and purposefully lenient on a player who needed to be dismissed.

Have you left a nine-year-old player in the game because of the supposed "rule" that "you can't card a player under 10?" Wrong. If little Mikey is out there breaking legs, little Mikey leaves. Don't want to send Mikey? OK, here's the rest of the conversation: "Well, your honor, the lawyer is right that I should have sent Mikey off for violent conduct after the second broken leg, but I had always heard …" Finding for the plaintiff … you pay thousands of dollars in hospital bills.

Have you ever failed to report a player whom you cautioned or dismissed? That is a serious offense. The league or tournament is counting on you to submit a complete and factual report of the game, including misconduct. Accumulation of misconduct cards leads to suspensions. If you are not doing your job by reporting that misconduct, you are not keeping the playing field level. Even though the game you refereed included teams A and B, if B9 would have had to sit out the next game due to yellow-card accumulation, then your failure to report that yellow card has put team C at a disadvantage.

OK, here's the rest of the conversation: "Well, your honor, the lawyer is right that I should have sent Mikey off for violent conduct after the second broken leg, but I had always heard …" Finding for the plaintiff … you pay thousands of dollars in hospital bills.

Do you overprotect goalkeepers to avoid aggravation from defending players?

Look through Law 12 again. Look through all the Laws. If anyone can find a third passage that gives goalkeepers special privileges, let us know. Law 12 does allow the goalkeeper to handle the ball deliberately (within his own penalty area). It also gives a free kick to a team if an opponent prevents the goalkeeper from releasing the ball from his hands. That's it. There are many restrictions, but no added protection.

Just as with any field player, goalkeepers cannot be pushed, held, kicked or spit at. Opponents may not foul a goalkeeper carelessly or recklessly. If you hold the opinion that goalkeepers are granted or deserve some special coddling, speak with your mentors, instructors, assessors or association leaders. Certainly, you'll allow them to grovel for a ball on the ground at an attacker's foot — you wouldn't allow other field players to do that. But as a matter of Law, there is no special protection.

At the end of a match, do you exchange pleasantries with players who have made your 90 minutes a nightmare, or do you let them know it if they approach you?

Amazingly, referees do grip-and-grin with players who spent much of the 90 minutes directing abusive language in their direction, publicly doubting the referee's parentage and worse. At some point, enough is enough. At some point, however subtly, referees can send the message that the after the game let's-be-buddies greeting is not desired.

In some cultures, that is an expected part of the sport. Your options? *Referee* is not a fan of having referees move toward the center circle at the game's end. Meet as a trio near the referee's game-ending location and move toward the locker room. If you are at an open field, the recommendation is to keep your bags near a goalline, not between the benches. Observe the postgame exchange as you back away, toward your gear. If the "nightmare" player starts to approach you, wave to him from a distance as you move away, maybe mouthing the word, "Thanks." If that player continues to approach, hold up your hand in a stop-sign fashion and say something neutral like, "See you next time" or "Good luck next week."

If that doesn't work, and the player does actually approach you, don't be rude. Shake hands and offer a neutral comment. If the opportunity presents itself, talk to the coach. Express your dissatisfaction with the player's actions during the contest. Talk about the incident in your next association meeting. Let the rest of the area's referees know so they can take some preventive action in future contests. Make it clear that the match was not a pleasant experience as a result of this player's behavior and that the spirit of the game was much traduced.

At the end of the match, do you blow your whistle when your stopwatch shows time, or when the ball is in 'no-man's land?'
Either is acceptable. Just be consistent. Adopt a standard philosophical approach and do it the same in every game. In 20 years of teaching referee clinics, I've asked that question many times at recertification clinics. The split is about 60-40, favoring letting the ball get to some innocent place on the field. Make up your own mind. Don't let someone who has the other philosophy tell you they are right, according to the Laws. They may offer a convincing argument that you accept, but they can offer nothing in the Laws that supports their point.

Do you, as an assistant, give the ball out of play when the ball is say, half over the line, to suit players' and spectators' interpretation?
Much like the question above dealing with 10 yards, there are two reasons why you raise the flag in that case. Either you don't know the Laws well enough to know when the ball is out (whole of the

ball wholly crossed the goalline or touchline, whether on the ground or in the air) or you are giving in to pressure. Whether it's Coach Jones' pressure, or the screams of dozens of parents of young players, you are breaking the Law by raising the flag for a throw-in when the ball is half over the line.

If only those players and parents realized how insignificant that throw-in going to their team really is. In fact, it's usually detrimental at youth play. Here's an experiment for you to perform. At high school play or youth play below U-16, make a four-quadrant graph. Label the left side as team A, the right side as team B. Label the top half as "controlled throw" and the bottom as "did not control." Then while watching four games (so you have enough data), make a check mark in the top half when team A makes a throw-in and *both of the first two touches* are made by team A players. Make a tick mark in the bottom half when either of the first two touches is by a team B player.

If your data is anything like that collected in the past, about 55-65 percent of your tick marks will be on the bottom half of the page! Spread that word around and soon you'll have parents screaming, "No, ref. It's not our throw-in. It's theirs, really. It hit our kid on the way out. Please, ref, you gotta give them the throw."

Have you ever given a decision that you normally wouldn't have because you were being assessed?

There is an oil-company commercial that features a woman carrying a box and she says, "Do you change your oil every 3,000 miles? Trust us, guys, women know." Guess what, referees? Assessors know. You'll fool one or two. But the vast majority of the 1,800 assessors in the country are experienced referees. They've done the same tricks you think you're pulling on them.

For referees who understand assessing, the stated goal of an assessment is to make you a better referee. Assessors are taught to find you doing something *right*, so they can tell you about it and praise you for it. If assessors can find you doing a dozen things right and tell you those are proper actions, you can incorporate them into your overall game management and you will improve. Of the hundreds of actions you take and decisions you make during a game, isn't it comforting to know that at least 12 of them are proper?

So if you take actions or make decisions that are different than you would normally take if you weren't being assessed, you are only cheating yourself.

Have you over penalized a player for a misdemeanor you failed to punish him for in a previous game?

Players, fans and coaches only want consistency. (Well, they claim they want it, unless they are the team A coach and you're about to caution A6 for the same action that earned B4 a caution earlier in the game.) You may gain a reputation for being a sheriff (give a card at the slightest provocation) or as a pushover (your last card was during the Reagan White House). But teams have to know what to expect from you.

If you confuse them from one game to another, they are naturally going to say something to you about your shifting standards. Sometimes, they may even say it in an appropriate way. But more than likely, they will express their frustration in a dissenting manner. So, you now have two cards (the over-penalized player and the dissenting player) because you shifted your standards from one meeting to the next.

... The list is not exhaustive.

It may be that you have never consciously done any of those things. But if you have, does that make you a cheat? I have — under the guise of common sense — perhaps that makes me even more of a cheat!

That was the way they ended their thought-provoking article. Are you a cheat? I admitted to at least one past sin. Referees train and study and attend meetings and purchase equipment all in the hope of doing a good job. Is your training going to waste because you're not adhering to the Laws or competition rules? Are you overlooking key aspects of the Laws because it's the easy thing to do? Are you making up your own opinions and interpretations? Are you the inconsistent referee, the one who doesn't conform to the referees in your area that causes coaches to say all referees are inconsistent? Are you the lenient one? Hope on board!

The following are the remaining questions posed in the original articles. If you are mentoring a referee, ask that referee to write out their thoughts on these questions.

• *Do you ignore technical offenses knowingly, e.g., at the place kick, are players in their own half at start of play or is the ball correctly placed for corners?*

• *Have you ever failed to award a penalty kick because you decided that the offense was too trivial to justify 'an almost certain goal?'*

• *Have you ever given an indirect free kick in the penalty area for an offense that was clearly a penal offense?*

• *Do you always give offenses that occur on the boundary lines of the penalty area as occurring outside?*

• *Have you ever used advantage as an excuse for failing to make a decision?*

• *Have you ever played longer, or shorter, in a match in an effort to, shall we say, get a result?*

• *Have you ever used a club linesman as a scapegoat after the award of a dodgy offside?* (Editor's note: *In England, most youth and amateur matches have club lines actually request offside by raising the flag. Do not do that in matches played under USSF jurisdiction.*)

• *If a referee asks for constructive criticism, do you withhold comments in case they might offend him and affect your mark?* (Editor's note: *In England, each referee gives both assistants a rating from 1-10 after each game. That rating, along with the marks from each coach, go into your overall season rating. Those ratings determine who moves up to the next leagues.*)

Notes

4

Myths About the Laws

By Bob Wertz

Sonia Denoncourt, Canada

Mythology plays a part of everyday life and soccer's *Laws of the Game* are no different. The origins of many myths about the Laws are unknown but they tend to feed on themselves and take a life of their own, embraced by players, coaches and spectators. Unfortunately, those myths lead to misunderstandings or misinterpretations and become a source of complaint to soccer's administrators.

FIFA helped eliminate some myths when it thoroughly modernized the current laws by remolding them in plain English. Still, consider the following myths that referees encounter from game participants:

1. "But ref, I got the ball"

A phrase used by players to justify an infringement committed against an opponent before, during or after a play for the ball. The rationale used by the player is: "If I successfully get the ball, then anything else I do must be OK." Consider a typical game situation in which a ball is cleanly tackled by an opponent. However, in the next instant, the player cleverly hooks the opponent's foot, resulting in a foul. Here are two separate events — a clean tackle and a tripping foul that the referee whistles. Because referees are trained to observe tackles closely from beginning to end, they can separate the fair and unfair play and penalize appropriately.

> Consider a typical game situation in which a ball is cleanly tackled by an opponent. However, in the next instant, the player cleverly hooks the opponent's foot, resulting in a foul. Here are two separate events — a clean tackle and a tripping foul that the referee whistles.

2. No subs in the last five minutes

Some coaches, and referees too, believe that substitutes are not allowed toward the end of the match because that leads to time wasting. Allow substitutions as the Laws or rules of competition permit. However, there is no general Law or specific rule of competition that prohibits substitutions within the last few minutes of a half. If you believe there is time wasting, the *Laws of the Game* provides for added time. See *Advice to Referees* 3.6.

3. Two players at a dropped ball

One of the greatest myths about the game is that two players must be present at a dropped ball. The dropped ball is a method for you to restart play after a temporary stoppage. The only restriction on its use is that it not be done in the goal area. While it seems fairest to drop the ball between two players, it certainly is not a problem to drop the ball to one player whose team had clear possession before the temporary stoppage. That gesture by the referee would certainly be in the spirit of fair play as well. *Editor's note: NFHS 9-2-3 says, "The ball is dropped ... between two opposing players." However, in case of clear possession, 13-2-2L allows an indirect free kick to that team.*

4. All high kicks are dangerous

Many players and spectators at youth matches believe that all high kicks are unfair and unsafe. High kicks are not dangerous when no other players are near the kick. It's only when other players have their ability to play the ball hampered by the high kick of an opponent that it becomes a dangerous play.

5. Players cannot play the ball while on the ground

Similarly, when a player plays the ball while on the ground and it is not a danger to himself or an opponent, there is no infraction. When there are opponents around, then the actions of the player might be dangerous since the player on the ground may be kicked inadvertently. In that scenario, wait momentarily to determine if such a kicking situation develops — then quickly take appropriate action. *Editor's note: Under NFHS rules, you may call dangerous play if an act endangers a teammate.*

6. Punish little fouls by an indirect; punish big fouls by a direct

Those fouls are usually described that way by the uninformed: a little push in the back that causes a miss-header earns an indirect free kick; a shove that knocks the player down is a big push. The Laws make no such distinction. Penal fouls are infringements committed against opponents and punished with a direct free kick (or penalty kick if in the penalty area). Lesser infringements, such as offside and impeding an opponent (formerly obstruction), are technical in nature. Punish them by awarding an indirect free kick.

7. You must warn players before you caution them

Some players believe that a caution is a two-step process. At the first instance of misconduct, they believe that they must first be warned, and then, at the next instance receive a caution. It's easy to see why that gets misinterpreted. You observe escalation of unfair play by a player and subsequently warn that player to "back off," when the incident by itself required no caution. Players then incorrectly interpret that to mean they will always be warned in the future about similar play, before a caution. That is not always the case.

8. You must caution players before sending them off

A corollary to number seven is that players believe that a send off is also a two-step process for unfair plays. With FIFA's increasing emphasis on stamping out violent tackles and serious foul play, players should face the fact that attempts to hurt or maim opponents will find them sent off without a previous caution.

9. Second whistle at free kicks

Players train to take free kicks and to defend them. Many players believe that a second whistle is always necessary after the initial whistle for the foul. However, unless an attacking team specifically asks for 10 yards at a free kick, a team can take a free kick immediately after it's been awarded to them. Unfortunately, too few players capitalize on that situation, which is one of the best scoring opportunities there is in a game. Often, the referee becomes an accomplice in that myth by commanding the kicking team to wait for a second whistle while a defensive wall is set, even though enforcement of the minimum distance wasn't requested.

10. Shielding versus impeding

Many players confuse legal shielding of the ball with obstruction (impeding). As long as the ball is within playing distance (meaning, capable of being played), a player can legally shield the ball from an opponent. In such a case, there is no obstruction.

Even when a player runs with a ball for 10-15 yards until the ball goes out of play, players do not impede opponents as long as they stay within that short distance. In other instances, some players mistakenly believe they have been charged — when in fact they were obstructing, which led to the charging.

Those situations are just some of the myths that referees encounter.

(Bob Wertz, former chair of the USSF referee committee and current chair of the Louisiana Soccer Referee Committee, lives in Baton Rouge, La. This article first appeared in the Spring 1999 edition of Keeping in Touch, *the official magazine of the U.S. Amateur Soccer Division.)*

Notes

5

No Harm, No Foul

By M.C. O'Bryant

Sandra Hunt, FIFA referee
from Washington

ED PURCELL

In his book, **Making It As a Sports Official,** *M.C. O'Bryant explores the use of the "no-call" in officiating. Hated by some, loved by others, the no-call often evokes a passionate response from officials. Whether you agree or disagree with the thoughts O'Bryant offers, you should agree that as we continue to think, we continue to grow as officials, O'Bryant's philosophy is:*

No Harm, No Foul
By M.C. O'Bryant

The home team is down by a touchdown in the waning minutes of a state high school football playoff game. It's third down with the first-down marker a short three yards away. The quarterback starts his cadence when you notice the halfback's helmet buckle isn't completely snapped. That's a five-yard penalty in the rulebook. Are you doing the right thing by calling it? Do you look the other way instead? Sure, that's a football example, but there are equally viable soccer examples.

"Never," says John Arbogast, a baseball and softball umpire from Bloomington, Ill. "To keep sharp one must enforce the rules without passion or prejudice at all times." Arbogast's opinion isn't uncommon, nor is it universal. Many officials avoid the gray areas and work a game with the straight-forward philosophy of "a foul is a foul"; others attempt to identify acts prohibited by rule, then decide whether the infraction should be penalized.

An intelligent discussion requires defining first and foremost what a no-call is and the purpose it serves. A no-call is a conscious decision on the part of an official to ignore an infraction that, if called, would place the offended player or team at an even greater disadvantage.

An intelligent discussion requires defining first and foremost what a no-call is and the purpose it serves. A no-call is a conscious decision on the part of an official to ignore an infraction that, if called, would place the offended player or team at an even greater disadvantage.

That can pose problems for the official who knows the rulebook inside and out, backward and forward. It also creates problems for the inexperienced official who hasn't mastered the art of the no-call.

Quality officiating does not entail blowing the whistle every time an incidental infraction affords the opportunity. It is, on the other hand, the ability of an official to apply the rules with the same prudence and equity at all times while ensuring that neither team exploits the rules to gain an unfair advantage.

Such officiating is accomplished with a minimum of disruption to play. A lack of understanding relative to the concept of no-call gives rise to whistle-blowing officiating that takes the contest out of the hands of the athletes and transforms it into a symposium on rules trivia.

What makes the no-call such an anomaly is that in spite of its prominent role in officiating, it is mentioned in only a few of the rules-related publications. A clear concept may take years of officiating to master and, although it may seem to be a contradiction, no-calls are basic to journeyman-level job performance.

Jay Shaheen, a volleyball and softball official from Williamsburg, Conn., agrees. "Only veteran officials have earned the right (to make no-calls). The veterans know full well the potential consequences, and know how to explain themselves about their no-calls."

Despite the fact that most rulebooks and officials manuals do not refer to no-calls, recognition of the need for application of the concept is not new. Some sports do address the issue. Soccer, for instance, is one of the few sports that recognizes the no-call. Under *Advice to Referees* 5.5, it states the Laws of the sport are intended to create as few disruptions in play as possible. Soccer referees are instructed by the FIFA rulebook to "penalize only deliberate breaches of the law."

The late Oswald Tower, who served as editor and official rules interpreter of the basketball guide for many years dating back to 1914, was among the first to agitate for greater discretion on the part of officials in applying the rules.

A no-call is a conscious decision on the part of an official to ignore an infraction that, if called, would place the offended player or team at an even greater disadvantage.

The substance of Tower's officiating philosophy was, "It is the purpose of the rules to penalize a player who by reason of an illegal act placed the opponent at a disadvantage." The key phrase is, of course, "placed the opponent at a disadvantage." If the opponent is not placed at a disadvantage, then one has to question the wisdom of disrupting play when that can be justified only through the most literal interpretation of the rules.

In his book, *The Art of Officiating Sports*, John Bunn, former basketball coach at Colorado State College-Greeley, was even more emphatic in arguing for the official's prerogative in applying the rules. Although the term no-call was not used at the time his work was written, he deserves credit for stating the concept, if not for coining the phrase. The essence of Bunn's philosophy states: "It is not the intent that the rules shall be interpreted literally. Rather, they should be applied in relation to the effect that the action of players has upon their opponents. If they are unfairly affected as a result of a violation of the rules, then the transgressor should be penalized. If there has been no appreciable effect upon the progress of the game, then the game should not be interrupted. The act should be ignored. It is incidental and not vital. Realistically and practically, no violation has occurred."

That idea, sometimes stated as the "no harm, no foul principle," has withstood the test of time and remains one of the most viable working philosophies, among sports officials today.

An analysis of the following hypothetical case will provide a perspective of just how the concept of no-call works.

In a baseball game, the batter hits a sharp ground ball to the shortstop, who fields it and makes an easy-to-handle throw to the first baseman for a routine, and what appears to be uncontested, out. However, in the process, the first-base umpire detects what no one else saw: The first baseman removed his foot from the bag split-seconds before the ball entered his mitt. It can be argued that the first baseman was only clearing the baseline so as not to obstruct the on coming runner who appeared to be out by a good halfstride. The applicable rule here is clear: The first baseman must have the ball in his control before he removes his foot from the bag. However, the batter clearly did not get a hit and the early removal of the first baseman's foot from the bag was only to avoid any possible collision with the oncoming base runner. In view of the circumstances, in most leagues, such a technicality would be regarded as a no-call, and overlooked (perhaps prompting an unobtrusive umpire warning to the first baseman). Calling the runner safe in an instance such as this is an act of over-officiating.

It should be clearly understood that the intent of this section is not to explain what is or is not a no-call. Rather it is to acquaint the reader with that important but undocumented aspect of sports officiating. A clear concept of no-call may take years of officiating to master, and its mastery is a mark of journeyman-level job performance.

Anyone making a serious attempt to master the technology of sports officiating is well advised to begin with the study of the

"Comments on the Rules" section of the rulebook. The unit titled, "Basic Principles," is a guide for administering sports officiating rules. In that section of the rules, interpreters find their authority for making no-calls.

We're going to look at two different examples where, by rule, the referee was correct. But in each case, referees who take the correct action suffer a blow to their role in the game. The first comes from a boys' U-19 state cup semifinal. A shot, taken from 35 yards out, is going to sail about four yards wide of the goal. A defender, standing about 16 yards from the goalline (and about three yards from the referee) jumps at the ball hoping to head it away from the goal — not realizing it's off target. The ball skims his head and goes out of play. The goalkeeper runs to fetch the ball as all 21 other players set up for a goalkick. As the goalkeeper comes back with the ball, the referee signals for a corner kick. The referee has to convince 21 people he got it right. Only the referee, the assessor and the player hit in the head with the ball know the truth. The other 21 were very happy to restart with the goalkick. By rule, the referee got it right. But that's a no-call. Why work extra hard to convince 21 players they got it wrong and you got it right?

The next example is at a kickoff to restart play after a valid goal is scored. Law 8 says that all players must be in their own half of the field at the time of the kick. Realistically, that provision is seldom enforced. Of course, if a winger is 20 yards downfield, you must bring the kick back. But for the teammate to be eight inches into the other half waiting for the short tap on the ball, consider the no-call. The Law backs you up on bringing the ball back. But the players are frustrated — they've just been scored upon. They just want get the ball into play and tie the score. Their focus is on active play, not the restart. Are you serving the game in the best way by using precious seconds to order the rekick?

Since most no-calls have to do with contact situations, it is well to review just how the rulebooks treat that issue. In addressing the subject of incidental contact, the rulebook sets three cardinal principles that have become the basis for most no-calls.

• The mere fact that contact occurs does not constitute an infraction of the rules.

• Even though it may be vigorous, contact that is entirely incidental to an effort by an opponent to reach a loose ball or that may result when opponents are in equally favorable positions to perform normal defensive or offensive movements should not be considered illegal.

• Contact that does not hinder the opponent from participating in normal defensive or offensive movement should be treated as incidental.

The following is a list of situations wherein ignoring infractions and allowing play to continue will contribute to the spirit of competition by avoiding unnecessary disruption of play.

• The infraction can be ignored without objection or without placing either team at a disadvantage.

• A call would have the effect of penalizing the team that was violated by the incidental infraction.

• A call would serve no purpose other than to note that an infraction had occurred.

• A call would violate a longstanding tradition and understanding by players, coaches and others as to how the game is to be played.

• A non-correctable error has occurred.

• A correctable error has occurred, but the game has progressed beyond the point where legal correction can be made.

• Late calls where neither team has gained an advantage and a new play situation has already developed.

• Incidental infractions are committed simultaneously and neither team gains an advantage.

• An apparent infraction has occurred, but the official does not know what, if any, penalty to assess.

Much more than simply missing a call in a blowout game, effectively utilizing the no-call requires an official to focus on the larger picture; preserving the flow of the game without placing either team at an advantage or disadvantage.

(Reprinted from Making It As A Sports Official *[1991] by M.C. O'Bryant with permission from the National Association for Sport and Physical Education, 1900 Association Drive, Reston, VA 20191-1599.)*

6

Fouls for the Ages

By David Keller

Ken Mather, Carmel, Ind.

T he game of soccer involves thinking and using physical skills to perform in an emotional environment. The physical, emotional and thought processes develop in individuals over time and differ in players of different age groups.

Those differences should dictate to the referee how the *Laws of the Game* and spirit of the game should be applied. Effective referees modify activities based on the age group involved. Sometimes you will see those differences expressed in skill differences as opposed to age differences.

The material contained in the chapter defines physical, emotional and thought development of U-6 players through adults. It addresses how you may treat fouls, misconduct and restarts at various ages. Within these pages, experienced referees should be able to envision situations they witnessed at various age levels. Less-experienced referees can gain insight into the differences of age groups as they advance up the ages.

The *Laws of the Game* are designed for physically and emotionally mature individuals. The referee must learn to modify application of the Law to meet the physical and emotional abilities of the age group.

The *Laws of the Game* are designed for physically and emotionally mature individuals. The referee must learn to modify application of the Law to meet the physical and emotional abilities of the age group. Some soccer organizations, such as the American Youth Soccer Association (AYSO), specifically acknowledge those physical, emotional and thought process differences. They modify coaching content to meet the development stage of the player and train referees to acknowledge those differences in the application of the Laws. For example, limiting the use of advantage during U-12 contests is an acknowledgement of the emotional and thought development of the age group. Also, using dangerous play at the U-6 level, rather than a penal foul such as jumping at, addresses the intellectual level of the player. Neither of those is designed to change the game or eliminate the *Laws of the Game*. Rather, they allow the players to enjoy play and develop a more thorough understanding of the game by appropriate application of the Laws.

General guidelines

1. Place emphasis on the differences made in refereeing a match based on the age of the players. Those differences include:

• Enforcing fouls and misconduct.

• Treatment of restarts and other Law enforcement.

• The changing role of the referee from *teacher* at U-6 through more dispassionate law enforcement at U-19.

2. This material can be used in a variety of mediums, from special training during a scheduled meeting to training conducted as part of a "Soccer Fest" or other activity.

3. Instructors or presenters must identify the knowledge level of the audience as early as possible and react accordingly.

Material description

A matrix containing the development and soccer-specific aspects of the players at various ages is included within this chapter.

Keys.

1. Emphasize the difference in implementation and why it is implemented differently (developmental characteristics).

2. Understand under what circumstances a Law should not be applied to an age group if the league specifically enacts a formal modification or to shape the application of the Law.

3. Support the concept of the spirit of the game living within

the letter of the Law. Players must be allowed to grow into the game of soccer.

4. Discuss the role of the referee as a teacher at lower levels and be aware of the difference between a referee teaching and coaching. An example is using a phrase such as, "Remember, you may place the ball anywhere in the goal area for a free kick" is teaching. "Place the ball here and kick it to number 11," is coaching. In addition, reminders of inappropriate activities, such as pushing at the U-6 level or sliding on the ground at that level, can be presented as positive reinforcement and teaching proper behavior.

Pushing an opponent

U-6

No. Pushing is natural at that age. Here, referees should begin to *teach* players not to push.

U-8-10

Yes. The concept is introduced at U-8 and should be well developed by U-10. That foul should be called.

U-12-14

Yes. As player speed improves, pushes are common. Often that comes from a player beaten in a play.

U-16-19

Yes. Pushing is common by both players in a challenge. Incidental contact should not be punished. However, persistent action that gives one player an advantage should be called.

Holding an opponent

U-6

No. Like pushing, that is a common activity at that age. The referee begins to *teach* players not to hold.

U-8-10

Yes. Holding should be reduced at U-8 and eliminated by U-10. Call that foul, especially at U-10.

U-12-14

Yes. Tactical holding is now becoming evident.

U-16-19

Yes. Holding is common by both players in a challenge. Incidental contact should not be punished. However, persistent action that gives one player an advantage should be called.

Kicks or attempts to kick an opponent

U-6

Yes. The first thing players are taught is to not kick others. Players should be reminded, not called for the foul.

U-8-10

Yes. That aspect should be improving as they grow. Fouls should be called in most instances at U-10.

U-12-14

Yes. Kicking, especially at the backs of the legs, appears at U-12 and by U-14 can be planned and intentional.

U-16-19

Yes. Kicking after the play is more common. Kicks after successfully challenging for the ball are not unusual.

Trips or attempts to trip an opponent

U-6

Yes. A basic foul that must be addressed and called at the U-6 level.

U-8-10

Yes. That aspect should be improving as they grow. Fouls should be called in most instances at U-10.

U-12-14

Yes. As player speed improves, trips are more common. That is a result of a player being beaten in a play.

U-16-19

Yes. Tripping in the attack zone becomes common. At that point, dives also become evident.

Spits at an opponent

U-6

Not applicable. Many children are beginning to learn to spit. Usually it is not directed at the opponent or intended to be an objectionable act. Discourage the act through teaching and, if necessary, a "timeout" from the coach will help.

U-8-10

Yes. That act is highly unlikely except in accidental cases. However, players should understand the foul.

U-12-14

Yes. Like striking, the player should understand that foul.

U-16-19

Yes. Spitting at that age is malicious and should be considered misconduct.

Handling the ball deliberately

U-6

Yes. Only call a foul if they catch or pick up the ball. Otherwise give the player a quiet reminder.

U-8-10

Yes. At U-8, referees introduce the deliberate nature of handling. By U-10, players are aware of the foul.

U-12-14

Yes. Players at the U-12 level begin to employ handling as a tactic, especially during chest traps.

U-16-19

Yes. Handling as a tactic continues to be seen. Call hand-to-ball contact at that level. Avoid trifling infractions.

Jumps at an opponent

U-6

No. That level player will jump a lot and will fall into others.

U-8-10

Yes. Perhaps not at U-8, but by U-10, introduce the concept as the ball is more frequently in the air.

U-12-14

Yes. As the ball is played more in the air, heading skills are developed and jumping at is more common.

U-16-19

Yes. Jumping at an opponent when the ball is in the air is not unusual. In addition, undercutting (tripping) is also common. The referee must learn to distinguish between the two.

Charging an opponent carelessly

U-6

No. That concept is not understood at that level. Players will run through anyone to get to the ball.

U-8-10

No. Still too early for that concept. If there is a size difference, unfair charges may be dangerous play.

U-12-14

Yes. Tactical charging and physical one-on-one challenges for the ball become common. Call that foul.

U-16-19

Yes. Charges are now very strong and are occasionally violent. Charges are also more prolonged as players move down the field.

Strikes or attempts to strike an opponent

U-6

Not applicable, except in rare individual cases. A "timeout" from the coach will help.

U-8-10

Yes. At U-10, that begins to become evident. At that level, the players should know not to strike.

U-12-14

Yes. By U-12, the player should clearly know that striking is not permitted. Call that foul.

U-16-19

Yes. That should be called on all occasions and misconduct considered. Goalkeepers striking opponents with the ball begins to appear.

Tackles an opponent with contact before touching the ball

U-6

No. The concept is not understood. Players should stay on their feet. Falling to the ground may be dangerous play.

U-8-10

No. The concept is still unknown. Players should stay on their feet whenever possible.

U-12-14

Yes. Playing on the ground under control begins to appear at U-12. Warn players before fouls are called.

U-16-19

Yes. Slide tackles are common. Players often hit the ball and the opponent at the same time. Often the player will flick the ball and then contact the attacker. That should be called as either dangerous play or kicking.

Dangerous play

U-6

Yes. That is often a catch-all for play at that level. If it looks dangerous, probably blow the whistle.

U-8-10

Yes. That infraction continues to be a catch-all. Call other fouls based on your ability to differentiate.

U-12-14

Yes. That call becomes less common as you call other fouls. High kicks and playing on the ground are common.

U-16-19

Yes. Dangerous play is rare. Most of the time, that can be seen when challenging for the ball.

Impeding the progress of an opponent

U-6

No. The concept is not understood.

U-8-10

No. The concept is still not understood.

U-12-14

Some. The concept begins to be understood. At that age group, warnings will be most effective.

U-16-19

Yes. Impeding is now done in a tactical situation to control the ball by a player or for a teammate. Impeding is also common on plays around the goalkeeper. That foul should be called.

Goalkeeper taking more than six seconds

U-6

No. Generally, there are no goalkeepers.

U-8-10

No. Goalkeeping begins to be introduced at U-8 and goalkeeper skills are introduced at U-10. Goalkeepers are usually a rotated position with limited skill development. Only at U-10 should a reminder of seconds be given.

U-12-14

Yes. Goalkeeping is now a primary position for a player. Warnings should begin at U-12 and, if flirting with the six-second limitation persists, a rare call should be made.

U-16-19

Yes. Goalkeeping is now a nearly exclusive position for a player. No more than one warning, at the first occurrence, should be given to the goalkeeper.

Goalkeeper making an illegal second touch

U-6

No. Generally, there are no goalkeepers.

U-8-10

No. Goalkeeping begins to be introduced at U-8 and goalkeeper skills are introduced at U-10. A foul may be called at U-10, usually after a warning.

U-12-14

Yes. Goalkeepers at that level should be aware of the infraction and it should be called.

U-16-19

Yes. Goalkeepers at that level should be aware of the infraction and it should always be called.

Goalkeeper handling a deliberate "passback"

U-6

No. Generally, there are no goalkeepers.

U-8-10

No. Goalkeeping begins to be introduced at U-8 and goalkeeper skills are introduced at U-10. A foul should be called at the U-10 level, usually after a warning.

U-12-14

Yes. Goalkeepers at that level should be aware of the infraction and it should be called if the kick was clearly intended for the keeper. Kicking skills are still not developed to a high level and mis-kicks are common.

U-16-19

Yes. Goalkeepers at that level should be aware of the infraction and it should be called if the kick was intended for the keeper. Kicking skills should be well developed and mis-kicks are uncommon.

Goalkeeper handling throw-ins from teammates

U-6

No. Generally, there are no goalkeepers.

U-8-10

No. Goalkeeping begins to be introduced at U-8 and goalkeeper skills are introduced at U-10. A foul should be called at the U-10 level, usually after a warning.

U-12-14

Yes. Goalkeepers at that level should be aware of the infraction and it should be called.

U-16-19

Yes. Goalkeepers at that level should be aware of the infraction and it should be called.

Goalkeeper wastes time

U-6

No. Generally, there are no goalkeepers.

U-8-10

No. Goalkeeping begins to be introduced at U-8 and goalkeeper skills are introduced at U-10. Players at the U-10 level should be warned.

U-12-14

No. At that level, the infraction is very rare. The player should be warned and rarely called for that foul. Listen for direction from the bench and if the coach directs the keeper to waste time, then whistle the infraction.

U-16-19

Yes. Tactical timewasting is not common. Quick, early warnings should be employed and then a foul called. Again, avoid trifling infractions.

Prevent the keeper from releasing the ball

U-6

No. Generally, there are no goalkeepers.

U-8-10

No. By U-10, the referee should remind players not to prevent the keeper from putting the ball in play.

U-12-14

Yes. It is rare at that level and warnings are usually effective.

U-16-19

Yes. The players now know that is a foul. Usually one warning will be sufficient.

Cautionable offenses

Unsporting behavior — Dissent — Persistent infringement — Delaying the restart — Not respecting the required distance — Enters or reenters the field — Leaves the field

U-6

Not applicable. Any misconduct behavior should be dealt with by the coach using a "timeout" if necessary.

U-8-10

Not applicable. Misconduct should be dealt with using substitutes, especially at the U-8 level. However, in rare cases when a caution or send off is warranted, cards should be shown in as unobtrusive and non-threatening manner as possible.

U-12-14

Yes. At that level, misconduct should be rare. Talking to players, talking with the whistle, calling fouls for lesser degrees of contact and warnings usually are sufficient. If a caution or send off is warranted, cards must be shown.

U-16-19

Yes. Misconduct becomes more common at that level. Those players test the referee and "push" as far as they can. Whistling infractions, verbal warnings and the referee's personality are required to manage a match. Near the end of the management spectrum are cautions and send offs.

Throw-in

U-6

Retry if provided in league rules. Coaches work on that and need support. Usually allow any number of retakes, based on local league adaptations. Do not change players attempting the throw-in.

U-8-10

No retry. Reminders and instructions are appropriate. At U-10, illegal throw-ins should be called.

U-12-14

Yes. At that level, a throw-in should be well understood and accurately executed. Call violations.

U-16-19

Yes. The throw-in should be automatic. Trifling on location or technical matters should be avoided.

Goalkick

U-6

Get the ball in play by helping players. Don't change a player who cannot execute a proper kick.

U-8-10

Get the ball in play, but make certain that it clears the penalty area.

U-12-14

Yes. That should now be automatic and correct.

U-16-19

Yes. That is automatic.

Corner kick

U-6

Get the ball in play by helping the players. Don't change a player who cannot execute a proper kick.

U-8-10

Get the ball in play. Begin to make sure the 10 yards are given.

U-12-14

Yes. There are tactical considerations. Pushing for position is common. Verbal warnings should be sufficient.

U-16-19

Yes. That is now one of the highest risk goal-scoring opportunities. Gamesmanship and tactical pushing are common. Impeding the goalkeeper and other fouls must be carefully watched.

Ball placement on restarts

U-6

No. Get the ball back in play.

U-8-10

No. Get the ball back in play.

U-12-14

Some. Throw-in location and free kicks in the attacking third of the field should be correct, but not trifling.

U-16-19

Yes. Players will use ball placement to their advantage and care should be taken to insure fairness.

Advantage

U-6

Not used.

U-8-10

Not used except in rare occasions.

U-12-14

Used to some degree, but only when a clear advantage is seen.

U-16-19

Commonly used.

Offside

U-6

Not called.

U-8-10

Usually called, based on local league adaptations.

U-12-14

Always called, with care taken to insure participation.

U-16-19

Always called if there is participation. Participation is very important. The offside trap is now employed.

Notes

7

Ecstasy: Traveling to a Tournament

By Carl P. Schwartz

DALE GARVEY

Front – Rex Osborne (Bermuda), Alan Snoddy (N. Ireland),
Stanley Lover, author "Association Football Match Control",
Brian McGinlay (Scotland), Marco Dorantes (Mexico)
Standing – Bob Evans (USA), Ben Fusco (Canada), Abraham
Klein (Isreal), Malcolm Moffatt (N. Ireland), Ed Bellion (USA),
Gordon Hill (Scotland).

Traveling to attend a tournament is pure ecstasy to a referee trying to learn the craft. I have long advocated that traveling out of your home area to attend a tournament is worth an entire season's worth of experience in your local youth league.

Do you know what an expert is? Anyone, more than 50 miles from home. If you travel 200 miles to referee at a tournament, none of the teams are aware of the mistakes you've made in the past. They don't know that last year you were lazy, but over the winter you made a firm commitment to improve your refereeing skills. They don't know that you've had a historical problem knowing when to display a misconduct card. All they know about you as you get ready to do their game is what you show them as you walk to the pitch.

Properly dressed? Arrive at the field well before the game? Have both assistants with you? Seen to be engaged in a professional discussion with the assistants? Walking the field as a trio? Greet both coaches momentarily with a handshake, a quick word about agreement on the starting time and any simple game management requests? (For example, "Coach, your keeper will have to change jerseys. The orange is too close to the other team's red.") They can only expect a professional job. It may take them 10 minutes and four or five decisions on your part to insure they continue to have that expectation.

Socks around your ankles and shirt untucked? Smoking a cigarette or spitting out some chew as you talk to both coaches?

I have long advocated that traveling out of your home area to attend a tournament is worth an entire season's worth of experience in your local youth league.

Standing around and juggling the ball for three minutes as both teams await the coin toss? Even if you're right from your very first call, the teams are on you from the get-go. You've set a tone that you are not up to their standards. They also traveled to get there — paid a lot of money. They came to win a trophy or to hone their skills for State Cup or regionals. The teams don't want some referee who is obviously just out there for the bucks to mess up their chances or allow one of their teammates to get injured.

How do you get the most out of the experience?

Some tournaments are better than others. Some tournaments attract large numbers of teams without caring about the quality of those teams. Other tournaments turn away some teams that have not proven to be capable. Some tournaments work hard to build brackets that match competitive levels — Blue, Silver and Gold divisions within an age bracket. Those are important considerations for you as a referee.

If you are less experienced, you want those large tournaments with unevenly matched teams. Assignors know they can put you in the center of a match, with two experienced assistants, and let you administer the 10-1 drubbing in round-robin play. By the time the semifinals roll around, you'll be an assistant to an experienced referee.

If you are experienced and want to get much better, you might have to travel a further distance to attend one of the premier tournaments. They limit the teams to those with dominant win-loss records, past state champions or historically competitive teams over a decade-long period. They'll bracket the teams so even opening-round games are tough matches. Tournament assignors may check your bona fides with your local assignor or SRA.

How do you know where to go? Years ago, there was only word-of-mouth and the once-a-month Tournaments section of the weekly publication *Soccer America*. Those are still two of the best sources. Many states publish a newsletter that is mailed to all registered players and referees that often contains a page listing upcoming tournaments within the state. In the web-age, many states also have that information on their youth website. If you wish to travel to a neighboring state, you can look up tournament information on the Internet. Be sure to ask permission from your SRA to referee outside your state border; it's important for insurance purposes and to make sure your home state has games covered before releasing you. That's usually only an issue for top-grade referees.

To do that research on the web, go to www.ussoccer-data.com/pubtopic.htm and follow the links through "Get Topic List" and on to 0-76 "State's Web Page Addresses." Find the state you are interested in and see if it has a tournament listing. Many do.

Set some goals

You don't have unlimited time and you probably don't have an unlimited budget. Early in the season, plan your tournament involvement. When I lived in northern California in the early 1980s, unit president Lyle Gisi and I would plan to take flight at least five weeks in 12 during the summer. We would contact the tournament director and the referee assignor, and see if they wished to have us join them for their upcoming tournament. We would ask if other unit referees could fly in with us. Sometimes we traveled with as few as three referees, sometimes as many as six in Gisi's small private aircraft. All the arrangements were made at least six weeks prior to the tournament. If you say you're going to go — go! Again, remember to get your SRA's permission if you cross a state border.

Why are you traveling? What are you hoping to learn? Those referees who do a viable self-evaluation during their career gain more than their compatriots do. What are your weaknesses? What do you need to work on? Plan those needed improvements. "OK, in Denver, I'll work primarily on whistle technique. Two weeks later in Seattle, my focus will be recognizing the passing lanes. In July, I'll work on airborne challenges and finish up with body language and signals during the premier tournament in Las Vegas." You're still refereeing tough, competitive, hard matches, but you have a single focus on a single point of emphasis. It's a weakness you are trying to improve.

Get invited

It all starts with getting a name and phone number or e-mail address. Use *Soccer America*, use the Internet or use word-of-mouth from other referees who attended the tournament last year. (The first one or two tournaments are tough to get an invitation. Persist. During those early tournaments, you will make enough contacts that it will become very easy. As you establish your credibility, the tournaments will be contacting you!) Make them want you to come. Build a resume that shows what you've accomplished so far. Early in your career, the resume may only have the dates of your entry-level class and the instructor's name, the fact that you worked a single local-league tournament and maybe a Developmental and Guidance assessment. If you received some good comments on that assessment, send along a copy.

By your third year, you can add the dates of your recertification training, maybe a State Cup early-round game and an assignment as an assistant on the local tournament semifinal. It may not be much — but it's telling the assignor at the other end that a few assignors in your area trust you to work the important matches. If you upgrade, include it. If you are starting to work high school varsity matches, use it. If folks have asked you to join your local NISOA chapter, include it. By now, you may have had a formal assessment. Again, if the assessor made a comment like, "Ready to handle tougher matches," be sure to mail a copy of that assessment along with your soccer-specific resume.

Provide information about other people who will sing your praises. Ask the tournament assignor to call your local assignor — provide a phone number or e-mail address. Ask ahead of time if your unit president will give you a positive recommendation. Include that phone number as well.

The Plano (Texas) Labor Day Tournament does just that. It won't accept any referee who won't provide that information — assignor's name and e-mail. They actually check. See the 2/01 issue of *Referee* for the full story on the Plano Tournament.

Ask for what you want

There are not enough referees who ask for what they want. There are referees who ask, but ask for the wrong things. There are referees who mistakenly ask exclusively for boys' U-18 centers, and want six of them in a day. There are referees who state they won't come to a tournament unless they get at least seven games each day. They're easy. They stay home and work the local league, because they're not invited.

If you are new to the tournament scene and would like to get some written feedback, ask to be assessed. Many tournaments are starting to assess referees who come. That's an added expense to the tournament, but it's also a drawing card to attract referees. If you want to be assessed and know that you can get free feedback about your capabilities, you might be more inclined to make that 200-mile drive. Some of the "better" tournaments are bringing in a staff of three, five or 10 assessors. You may not get a full scored assessment, but it's great feedback to help you improve.

If the tournament does not offer a formal assessment (either scored or Developmental and Guidance), ask for some written feedback from an experienced referee. Getting a scored assessment out of state takes some legwork. You do need prior approval from your state's state director of assessment (SDA), who will usually contact the other SDA. You will need an assessor of the appropriate grade for what you are trying to accomplish. While focusing on you for a full game, the tournament loses that assessor's services for other partial games, so they may not be eager to offer that service. But if you make the arrangements, it can happen.

Explain that you would like that written statement so that future tournament assignors in other areas will know how and where to use you. A statement such as "Ready for anything up to U-18 line and U-15 center" is golden to future tournament assignors. If that statement comes from a qualified assessor or a respected senior referee, you've got your invitation to the next tournament. (Again, you may think it's a small point, but many times those senior referees and assignors see each other at state high school championships or collegiate contests. They develop a trust in one another and their recommendation is usually heeded.

It is not a carte blanche for you to get a recommendation and then go screw up your next three assignments. But it gets your foot in the door and gives you the opportunity to prove yourself.)

If you are an experienced referee, but there is an element of your game that has not had a lot of experience, ask to be exposed to it. Early in my career, the competitive bug bit me. It didn't matter what age group or gender, I just wanted the toughest matchups offered — the two rivals that don't like each other. I wanted the match between two teams that had to be abandoned last year when they played. I wanted the rematch between the two teams that met two weeks ago in State Cup and the underdog won.

You may not see a lot of ethnic soccer in your area. Ask for some games involving various ethnic mixes. And ask for an assistant referee from one of the ethnic groups to give you some feedback at halftime and after the game is over. Two games involving Serbian players won't make you an expert on Serbian soccer, but when you see that ethnic mix in your first State Cup semifinal five years from now, you won't be surprised.

A few paragraphs ago, we talked about referees who ask for seven matches or four top age-group centers in a single day. Instead, ask for breaks. Ask for a chance to sit down. Ask for a chance to have an hour off to go sit in the referee tent and absorb some of the knowledge you've just gained. Ask for time to get off your feet, change your socks, get hydrated and recharge your mental batteries. Assuming shortened-half games and a mixture of older and younger age groups, you never want to exceed two games, break, two games, break and one game. You would probably do well to limit yourself to line, center, and line take a break and then one last center. Harried assignors will ask you to do more. There will be "just one more line. It's a girls' U-13. You can do it." Politely turn them down.

Why the break?

If you are traveling to tournaments to learn and enhance your referee reputation, you don't want a team seeing your performance on your seventh game of the day. If you tell them, you seem like a money-grubbing sort they could see back home. Not good. If you don't tell them, they don't care that it's your seventh game, they just know you're a terrible referee who can't keep up with play and has terrible concentration. Also not good.

The referee tent

That's where it all takes place. That's where all the learning comes into focus. As an experienced veteran of any referee tent will tell you, only believe about half of what you hear! But it's your chance to ask questions. It's your chance to explore the what-if-I-had-done alternatives and get feedback. You may be a sheriff as a referee. As you explain a game situation, a humorous referee or a laid-back referee may offer alternatives based on their styles that might benefit you in future contests.

You may have been questioned about a ruling. A screaming coach or loud parent may have given you pause based on a restart decision. As you talk about the play in the tent, someone will have an authoritative answer. More than likely you got it right, but should your ruling have been incorrect, an experienced veteran will explain the proper interpretation and should offer proof in the *Laws of the Game, Guide to Procedures* or *Advice to Referees*.

Listen. If you are good enough to be traveling to tournaments, you are probably considered among the top referees back in your local area. You're probably the one with all the stories. Everyone probably listens to you as you offer tips or techniques. If you truly are trying to get better, why spend valuable time talking about what you already know? Why not hush your face and let someone else educate you?

Ask for help

As you introduce yourself to your referee partners, tell them what you are hoping to learn. Tell them briefly about your point of emphasis and ask for feedback. "Bruce, Nancy, I'm really trying to focus on my whistle technique all weekend. I'm trying to talk-with-the-whistle with each foul I see. So if you have any specific feedback about a whistle that didn't match the severity of the foul, just touch the tip of your nose. I'll remember the incident and you can give me your thoughts at halftime or after the game."

Youth referees working with adult assistants

That is a challenge that rapidly advancing youth referees have to overcome. You might be teamed with an adult assistant because the veteran needs a rest from the physical demands of centering a match. You might be centering a tough match and the assignor has put an adult with special skills or a special personality to calm a known abusive coach.

But the scale has a balance — and too few youth referees know where that balancing point is located. You are in charge of that match. For those 70, 80 or 90 minutes, you are the leader of that referee crew. Act like it. Lead the discussion. Tell them what mechanics they should use to best suit your game and your needs.

Then, when the game is over and the crew is well away from coaches, players and spectators, the adult may offer some constructive pointers. You go from leader to student. But during the match, go into the game with the mindset that you are the leader.

One thing to avoid

In some areas of the country, assignors are lazy. They want to make one call and after that one call, they know they will have a four-person crew that will rotate and cover a field all day long (line, center, line, rest). That's easy for them. About 10 phone calls like that, and their tournament assignments are covered. They call the crew chief and the crew chief is responsible for putting together a four-person crew, finding out availabilities, etc. But that's not good for the referees. To some degree, you get a comfort level with those on your crew and you can anticipate their movements, signals and moods.

But if four of you from one area drive 200 miles to go to a tournament and team up as a four-person crew and work one field all day long — why didn't you just stay home and do that?

There are several tournaments that run from Dec. 26 to Dec. 31 in Florida each winter. If three or four of you are going to fly from your locale to work one of those tournaments, don't you want to work with other referees from other areas? Don't you want to see referees from other ethnic groups? Don't you want exposure to someone whose mechanics are slightly different? Don't you want to sit in the referee tent and listen to some new stories instead of hearing the same stale stories time and again? Don't you want to listen to how referees from the snow-bound north deal with horrible weather conditions? Yes, you do, in case you're from

Arizona and the morning you wake up for your State Cup semifinal — and it's 33 degrees with a 20-mph wind.

Tournaments are a great place to learn. Sometimes you may learn by watching what *not* to do. Sometimes you'll meet up-and-coming referees who will be top performers in the far-off future. ("Who's the referee for today's MLS match? Larry! Heck, I knew Larry back when he was a young state referee back in 2004.") In many cases, you will make friends who will stay by your side for decades. You may make professional and business contacts that lead to contracts and expanded business.

Get invited. If you're invited and pledge to attend, go. Tell the assignor and referee partners about the areas you're trying to improve. Sit in the referee tent during your breaks. Listen. Enjoy.

Notes

Notes

The National Association of Sports Officials

• NASO's "Members Only Edition" of *Referee* magazine every month. Members receive 96-pages of *Referee* with 16-pages of association news, "members only" tips, case plays and ducational product discounts.

• Members receive a *FREE* educational publication valued up to $9.95.

• Discounts on NASO/*Referee* publications such as the Officials' Guidebooks, rules comparisons and sport-specific preseason publications make you a better official.

• Referral service in the event you move to another community.

• Web page and e-mail communications keep you updated on NASO news, services and benefits.

• "Ask Us" rules interpretations service.

• Sports-specific rules quizzes.

• Free NASO e-mail address.

• Free access to the *NASO LockerRoom* — an NASO cyberspace service.

• Membership Certificate and laminated membership card.

• NASO Code of Ethics.

For a complete brochure and membership information contact:
NASO • 2017 Lathrop Avenue • Racine, WI 53405
262/632-5448 • 262/632-5460 (fax)
naso@naso.org or visit our website at www.naso.org

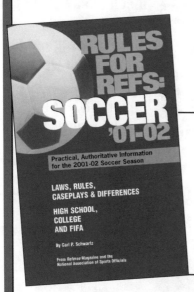